I0813508

PERVERTS

PERVERTS

KAY GABRIEL

NIGHTBOAT BOOKS
NEW YORK

Printed in the United States
Second Printing, 2026

ISBN: 978-1-643-62294-1

Design and typesetting by Kit Schluter
Typeset in **ACUMIN VARIABLE CONDENSED**, DIDOT LT PRO,
& LTC Goudy Oldstyle Pro

Cover art: Adaptation of Robert Maguire's cover illustration
for *In the Shadows* by Joan Ellis (New York: Midwood Books, 1962).

Cataloging-in-publication data is available
from the Library of Congress

Nightboat Books
New York
www.nightboat.org

CONTENTS

for Patrick

PERVERTS

1.

We developed a program of eliminating other people's eyelashes
First we did it by accident, as in I burned
my own off while trying to sleep
                                        Then we did it for justice, and then
for vigilante revenge   Open
the doors of perception we said, approaching
strangers and taking their eyelashes
it's Byronesque!
                                                    only in the dream we said debyronic
Christian my conspiratorial eyelash thief has not
yet sent me his dreams
Christian this is where your dreams will go in this canto
of an epic poem stitched together from the dreams of
friends or strangers, delegates
of the dream assembly
                                        who writes an epic poem in the 2020s? Perverts
                                                    luckily I'll quit after some pages
I'll backdate the poem to obscure my reckless
poor and still unashamed decisions

Reckless I sort through my revolutionary grammar
I do it in two big bins
One is for always repeating myself
one is for getting in trouble if I do it poorly
then I've gone to visit my mom in the Arctic
although it's December there isn't any
ice, she's on a boat docked in harbour
periodically she leads marches
    on the mainland rocking
the suburbanites off the balls of their feet
neither of us is well liked
    I walk in the sun around stupefied
blonde mothers and children and somehow
return to the water, where an ex crashes
the dream with an unfinished cowritten poem from
the period of our love covered
        in taunts and trenchant phrases
        pointed questions, points of order
        and accusatory dots all over the page humiliating,
        under the circumstances, to be asked
        my theory of power, and so bluntly

And by an enemy lover.
Then I'm on an interminable march
to a coded destination. There's a chase,
there's cops, there's friends.
I'd walk into traffic for them
if I had to, but why do I have to?
I mean why now, and for a hidden purpose.
A thick cluster shouts for power. We briefly
command the attention of the cars,
then the attention of the *Post*.
Then one of us exits the dream for Connecticut,
not before the headline writers get
a really good slander in, one of their best.
V and I have our photos taken in matching hats
we were supposed to look like celebrities
in a stairwell under cold light after arguing
all night dressed in garments
from an infamous sweatshop under the Williamsburg
Bridge. Mel Brooks arrives, he's the mayor,
we're allegedly sorry and won't do it again
payments coming due on bad decisions
"recklessly" making out and writing about it on
the wrong side of the day

Reckless I guess the word for public
health decisions a lover made
about his body conjunct mine
according to his roommates and his Tinder crush
I could litanize the shit I know, my questionable
choices and getting rawed on that
occasion would make the cut only
cause it happened on a half-
inflated blowup bed   he shot in my mouth
still, fuck fate and villainy   I remember
the sore throat a doctor insisted had to be the clap
and which friend was falsely informed in case of a fever
that he must have been seroconverting? I forget,
so we get to talking pills and diagnoses

Mike skimmed off the melatonin
I left at his house and Stephen asked
if Mike had any T he could part with   I said I dunno but I do
C. and his medical-grade ketamine I called my chemical blanket
M. who couldn't drink on Wellbutrin, but did
A. who hated her antipsychotics to extreme consequence
R. who rearranged her life for Ativan
B. who passes off his Klon like Juicy Fruits
the girl who bagged her Oxy and threw it in the trash
the girl who stopped taking Atripla
the girl who pushes her Adderall on party friends, they use it for work
the people's Lexapro, PrEP, Propranolol,
Valacyclovir
I'll leave some room for yours in this combination epic poem-Rx sheet

____

____

yours, the Doctor Perverts

in a world in which a pervert's as good as a doctor
as fastidious as gnarly as intrusive in attention
        Dee's on prazosin   a drug
I took for excess nightmares
its effects discovered from double-blind
trials on U.S. soldiers returned
from Iraq and Afghanistan   mine
made me faint in Colorado and Dee says
it traps them awfully in sleep   now Adam's
dreaming B movie horror shots:
a bird man in a plague mask walks with a cane
slowly under a streetlamp and "fucking charges
at the camera"   on another night blob
men lure you into a no-exit cult
I'd be entertained to appear as the final
girl of someone else's slasher
dreams but I guess only the dreamer gets out alive
and then only in the role of the camera

later I dream of three oversexed
teen vampires, real teenagers
who grow and change not just
Edward Cullen teenagers   I'm one of them
a boy vampire older brother younger sister   our mom
who we live with on a stage exposed
to the rain loves to trot us out in front of strangers
and expose our truly proficient
talent   it's Vampire Sondheim's Vampire *GYPSY*
one of her friends says she has permission
to come up and film us while we wake naked
from our vamping orgy so I say I'd rather
be blinded than filmed
                I demonstrate my preference
                temporarily blinding all three of them and restoring
                their eyesight, my brother who's also my lover
                        says: "No, not fair, I'll blind you, you price your
                point" and claws out our eyes, restoring our sight
                by incanting that it's "all fine now"
                the only evidence of the blinding is some black pus-
like gore but still I say *see* that was *awful*

As awful as the prazosin sleep?
I didn't ask. My dreams for
years were mostly awful: shouting
matches and unanesthetized
surgery, cartoon monsters in 90s
prosthetics, and unwinnable fights.
Then they were gaggy, theatrical,
and full of lessons, nightly
Lehrstücke.

From Jack Spicer's Martian, the one who
rearranges the mental furniture? Patrick, from you?
You fell off a roof in a dream I had, in 2024,
onto a platform I couldn't see, making the
gentle pose we struck together when Kyle dyed us
in the Pines, the one I called a trust fall onto fabric.
I approached and there you were, safely caught
and smiling. I knew the fort-da shit you were onto and still
my heart flew out of my mouth, ready to tumble
off the roof with or after you, as if
that would fix the fall   like when I say "I would walk into
traffic for"   when your husband says "I would
get rid of a body for—"
which I've adopted   a saintly practice?
Sure. Does it have to be?

Capri dreams it's the morning of his surgery
it's not like my anaesthetic-liberated nightmares
less terror, more confusion:
"We can't start the operation," the doctors explain,
"until you roll a cigarette"
Capri has to draw his own blood,
mix it with tobacco, drop it in
the cigarette paper, roll a perfect cigarette
but he stopped smoking for surgery,
couldn't roll any longer and didn't
want to draw his own blood either, I mean,
come on   still he spent hours pulling
blood and rolling tobacco damp with his
own discharge trying to force his failing
doctors to administer to him by night
like mine did in grade school   a recurring
dream of a doctor who was also a friendly
cuttlefish in a lab coat   you know the one in *Star
Wars* who shouts IT'S A TRAP
like that   maybe his brother

It's twenty-two years later
I'm in the lobby of a Toronto
hospital renamed after a millionaire's son
the hospital lobby is octagonal and I'm the tall
man in the white suite, the villain
developer in *Chinatown*   Faye Dunaway's
father   the water thief who reshapes
LA like and unlike Robert Moses carving up
the planet for the BQE   Seva thinks it's his best work
we live in Greenpoint and depend on it,
so it's hard to disagree   as if I'm
Patrick marveling at industrial society, all creation
treated in a single sewage plant
in the dream I'm accompanying a slight woman
we walk out of the octagon and into one of the
hospital wings, where my grandfather's
lying in bed waiting to breathe on his own
Chinatown at best an accurate fiction
the melodrama is sort of distracting and gratuitous
when the real drama is in the water supply!
still the makeup on Dunaway's blown-out head makes
her look like a painting clutching the wheel at 10 and 2
as artful and saturated as the *Alien* chestburster
scene but doing gender in a classical way

Jo, Chicago Jo, dreams of an unavailable
crush interrupting them with fond
taunting wishes, it goes like this:
        they're in a Stop & Shop
        they're searching for tea up and down
        the aisles, they find coffee and chocolate
        pop tarts, Clif bars but no tea
        run into their former district manager
        he gives them a hug and makes fun of their mullet
        talks to them about the new bosses
        suddenly Jo's starring in a procedural
Dear Jo: I guess you mostly dream of work? Years later
you walked into a combination Poetry Project
and restaurant job   you're fresh off a plane,
we're both talking to your boss   I make you
an extravagant Thanksgiving-themed sandwich,
"delicious, overly dry turkey"   your
boss distracts me   a coworker explains you have to retinol
your knees   I told him to buy a restaurant "outside of the city"
though it's not clear from context if we meant Chicago
or New York, two towns alike but not
identical in management

Jolene says her dreams all derive
from stress: as a child
she fell through the earth while shopping
for clothes or going to school
As an adult, she says, the dreams are more varied:
she's chased around her childhood
home, her lover rejects her, she can't
get people to leave her work after closing
time, complete a task like opening a door
or her legs won't let her walk, and sometimes
all these inhibitions clamp the same dream
for which reason she prefers not to dream at all
And I, who witnessed my midriff buzz-sawed,
I get it   organs on display, the daubed
gloves of a triumphant doctor   Seva reaches
across the bed and shakes me out of it
like he's Cher and I'm Nic Cage for once in our invert lives

Like love don't make things nice?
Rainer put me in their dogsitting dream,
in Ithaca, a fake one, a place dressed
as Ithaca for Halloween. It's accessible by taking
a train to a ferry to a train, there's a waterslide
river on the Hudson. We were together in grad
school, taking a quest-like field trip to the dogsitting
house over a bridge of mud and moving cliffs
the terrain threatens collapse under our feet.
We collected and lost a talisman.
I forgot to ask what the dog was like.
When the house was destroyed it whimpered
in the corner. Rainer hugged the dog, so I'd guess that,
whatever size or shagginess, it was pleasant to hug.
We threw a grad school party for completing the quest,
and that's where we lost the talisman. Rainer
grabbed a cardboard box instead and filled it
with whatever we wanted to steal: brown paper
lunch bags, embroidered with flowers. Then we taught
a class together, only Rainer lost their temper:
although they "snuck away to be bad," I paused
class until they returned, foiled their laziness,
forced them to teach. In Rainer's dreams
I'm an icon of patience, not a Macaulay
Culkin party monster, not a bitch who checked
Grindr instead of studying for quals and nearly,
ha ha, flunked out into a marriage fated to crack

Should I summarize? For you, Rainer, I kept
my infuriating cool. The dog
was saved, we taught our class,
we replaced the vaguely powerful talisman
with bespoke paper bags. Our students
left us rave reviews. No classroom
observers witnessed our inadequacy.
We didn't teach naked
or in compromised positions. Right-wing
radio ignored us. Rent-a-cops passed by.
Administrators railroaded other people,
not us. Not us. We had our jobs, and we performed
at them. We dissatisfied only each
other. Everything ended as dainty
as if the god of marriage in a comedy push-pinned
cheating spouses into place, and restored the kings

2.

In December I dreamt I was hospitalized
at a clinic but I broke out of it, sliding into a cold
landscape in other people's yards and land.
It's the Betty Ford clinic only it's in Vermont
I can tell cause of the snow and pine
needles and cause everything's cut
into triangles. There are deer but they
are secret. The hill I'm sliding
down requires secret deer language
and its owner, a friendly older white
man, comes home, but I don't trust him   instead I run
and hide in a copse and write a note
I later struggle to decipher   something about the snow
and sanctity of deer language, how you cannot use it to build
or slide down your triangular hill in the dark

At an art show or university,
Anu also dreams of prison breaks.
An organizer from Critical
Resistance presents research about "knots,"
which demonstrate the breakdown of structure
over time. There's a test:
he asks Anu what he thinks his conclusions
mean for the future. She despairs of it:
a scorched-earth end to things. Wrong,
he says: It means that prisons are, eventually,
going to be abolished

Is that a guarantee? It's faith. To prove
the point, Anu dreams two prisoners escape,
chased by two COs. One guard gives up,
the other persists: "dogged, old timey,
dedicated," after the escapees,
who run into a video game
chase across a lake. One escapee
can run on water, one steers
a machine. The CO swims,
not well or fast, but doggedly. The escaped
non-prisoners beat the game. Kate Moss,
now a labor organizer, walks by,
in her glitter body suit

And Connie dreams of New
York Yiddishkeyt   setting: the Bronx,
a cafe, a factory and lecture hall
her acquaintance or co-star and addressee
travelled to New York for archival
research   the two pass through
a neighborhood like where Connie's
grandfather moved from Poland   stop in a café
of Yiddish speakers drinking hot
sweet teas and clear liquors,
basically paint thinner, in tiny glasses
"you tried to make contact with
a labor organizer"   under
surveillance, the organizer allows
access to the archives where their family
history is stashed, a guarded file in a union
hall, old and crowded, unkempt really
loose documents on the shelves
in the dream Connie could read
Yiddish, so she cried
the two left the lecture hall "talking about like
socialism or unions or something"
my grandfather too briefly a socialist
architect before he left Apartheid South
Africa, moved to Montreal
and designed shopping
plazas and sometimes homes
I dreamt of a march proceeding
slowly to his house in Ottawa
it's the object of a protest and it's Ridgewood too
inside it's orange, large and medieval
I could call him now to ask about
his health and he'd only talk about Zero Mostel
who picked up Dick Cavett and waltzed
him the length of his own stage

like puppetry’s special goy
but I wouldn’t learn his
temperature or the state of his cough

Mike dreamt of a band named My Chemical
Abortion, then of asking his crushes
to reveal themselves but only coworkers
responded at the job he was trying to quit
          then he was living in the woods
once he dreamt he was walking himself on a leash,
                    did I get that right?
waking up I told you my head felt like a black
velvet bag   "What's in the bag?" you asked
"Nothing," I said first, then: "Monopoly money,
or counterfeit money," and finally: "Crimes"
                    Ro once had a night terror sleeping
          beside her former lover now moved
                    to Boston and gone stealth
          the lover sitting astride her became Luca Brasi
                    from the *Godfather* and choked her awake
I'm no night terrorist, I'm a fake Kay
like Diane Keaton in the *Godfather*
                    now who's naïve my husband's asking
in, of all places, dull New Hampshire
          all my outfits in part 2, that exquisite
coat I'm wearing when Al Pacino slams the door
in my face, make up for the wigs they made me wear
in part 1 where some of the Italians are actually
Jews like James Caan
                    I'm definitely naïve, Senators kill people
                    so do Presidents and Democrats
                    I'm an intense waif, née Adams
                    I'm God and this is my husband Michael
Warren Beatty casts me in *Reds* as I bundle
the Corleone kids in the back seat
and steal away from the 50s

I tease Ro for liking Jewish women
I ask her when she's gonna
convert but she says that would ruin the fun
of being the shiksa which is to say in dating us
Ray didn't care for *The Godfather* which she says
was mostly about men   fine, but I'm
fixated on the history (tragedy) of Europeans who
became white and I don't mind the movie's homosocial exchanges
of death, fruit, favors and crimes
I like men and villains
I like the romance of kissing your brother
on the eve of the Cuban Revolution
Christian, I lied, your dreams go here:

> once you dreamt that an unfamiliar
> coworker was giving out spray bottles of what
> you assumed to be weed, your boss gave you one
> and asked if you ever go shooting   you said yes
> when you play basketball
> later down a small-town street chased by young
> boys taunting you   when you tackled
> them you spoke with one who said
> his sister was Mary Shelley but she wasn't
> famous yet   the evidence: her brother
> didn't yet know *Frankenstein*

you sent me this dream and I nearly replied:
oh, you must have tackled Percy—
I stopped myself but Stephen says
in the Shelleys' letters they call each other brother and sister
so: I guess you kind of did
"Contemplating Hell," Brecht says,
"my brother Shelley supposed it would mostly resemble London"
as Brecht thought it'd be like LA
the brothers Brecht and Shelley kiss on New Year's
they join the revelers in the former banks, they surely would
now I'm your twin but I haven't written *Frankenstein*,
sunk into the mud at the Villa Diodati, miscarried
or done anything of note, I'm 17
or 27, I dream of wearing a harness and asking
to be hooked to something, nobody's listening
I say *hooked, hooked* but you don't get it
soon after I dream I'm lying rather innocently on your lap
and you're flicking hair off my face strand by brotherly strand

Then in January I dream of swimming in a polluted
river called the Say, which is and is not the Gowanus
Canal   I was and was not in the mob
I definitely had a boss with fat cheeks sat in a nylon
folding chair and I also dreamt about purges
I was a delegate in the National Assembly in 1789
our meetings took place in a pool, I lined up
brightly colored straws on plastic rhinoceros toys
I did it to represent caucus maneuvers
in the dream I was on acid and a very strong swimmer
the delegates swam in a bourgeois pool
I find a doll street artist, we make out selfishly
in the dreams I'm a little gayer than in waking life
often in water, surprisingly toppy
though I never did finish lining up the straws

So what would you do as a parish
priest in the 1780s in protest over the salt tax?
A scruffy Jacques Roux bound to himself
dreams of property as an athletic lover
Patrick you dreamt of the CUNY
Graduate Center library
on fire, you dove in to save Stalin's
copy of *Capital*
Ruthie arrives to congratulate
you for doing the right thing since,
she says, "He likely
never even read it anyway"
then the same week you dreamt of a mass
meeting of the Left, an old-school
gym or auditorium—I'm editorializing
here but I can see this combination general
assembly or Historical Materialism gathering:
white walls, movement egos
everyone's sitting on the floor in their million debates
David Harvey in his 80s addressing the assembly
says something that sets the factions at war
against each other and especially him
like either he bent the stick too far on
a useful, unfashionable point
or downplayed some real but minor critique—
a chorus of hundreds shouts and exits the dream
but you'd been given a job as his minder
it's your task to explain the debacle
to the confused and sad Harvey
he doesn't fully understand why
or how he instigated the split
then you took him back to the house you were renting
together, comforted him and put him to bed
logged onto Grindr and got caught
mid-fuck on the veranda with your app hookup
though not by David himself

I'd pay good money to see the caucus theater,
the burning library, Stalin's unread Marx
once you starred in a slightly too cinematic
dream I had in which a bearded Trudeau, Jr.
arranged in an end of history maneuver
for Ottawa to be secretly populated by robots
he hoped nobody would notice
and maybe nobody would have without,
Patrick, your role in the dream:
you hack the robots such that they stop
moving and start shouting horrible shouts
making such a tremendous
noise they upend the peaceable
and frankly boring capital where nothing
moves except speculation at the speed
of hoisting bitumen out of the ground
now it's a place of total noise
and chaos, shouting robot shouts
a noise show in a barn somewhere made
public like a social wage
C. had a Merzbow shirt from a show that
"caused him nerve damage"
when we dated I liked to wear it and pretend
I was the boyfriend, a punching bag for sound
though really I protect my delicate ears
Patrick I'm a sap for pretty shit
Brecht and Artaud make beauty
suspect as it should be
that's their real point of contact
now my broken doorbell is hissing
at the mouth like a robot in Trudeau
Jr.'s house of commons
or that parish priest urging arms over the salt tax
Ottawa has shed its clothes of bureaucratic perfection
in the dream the shouting
robots allowed something to unlock

elsewhere since Ottawa, here and always
a city of squares, was consumed
by its forever droning puppets and nobody died

And nobody died: optimism!
Well *I* think that's funny
I'm being dialectical so you don't have to
I lived with a guy who said: it won't be
a good revolution if I survive it,
fighting the people's war in Paterson, NJ
crisis escalated me out of that place
and into the expensive hovel, near the Home
Depot, with the roaches and the infuriating smell
the one long-lasting roommate an aging
beauty and a spy for the landlord
remember how I lived with Stephen and Liam
for a month to avoid her?
Then Stephen towered over my dreams like a nightly
impresario. Here's one he had about me:
"I'm at a restaurant with Kay," he writes.
"We join a table where Margaret Mead is sitting.
Kay is like is that Margaret Mead. She starts
going on super Margaret Mead-type rants. She
kind of looks like Joan Didion"—wait for it—
she starts talking about the last words of W.H.
Auden and transphobia. "Nobody's more
celebratory of the erotic than trans people,"
I said, in Stephen's dream, at the Margaret
Mead table, or did Margaret say it? Then I told
Margaret about "fucking boys' mouths on day 2
of affairs." "Day 2 is kind of a Margaret day":
In Stephen's writeup of this dream that's in quotes,
so either I editorialized to Margaret Mead about
dedicating the second, mouth-fucking day
of an affair to her, in quiet contemplation, like
a day in the French Republican calendar dedicated
to cabbage, or she inserted herself into my tawdry
affairs to self-dedicate mouth-fucking to the memory
of Margaret Mead and other Margarets. I thought

she was a Christian Socialist, I mistook her
for Dorothy Day. In the dream Stephen's holding
me and spooning me, he feels deep Platonic
love and then "Kay's also W.H. Auden and I'm crying
because I love him so much and I can't speak." W.H.
Auden is trans, like poetry is a way
of happening, like Brecht is a strange and useful
megabitch. Patrick says I'm reanimating
his interest in aesthetics, an "effete kitten
he'd long since drowned." Auden's last
words are a "kind of stuttering monologue
about beauty and gratitude throughout which
he gradually loses coherence." There,
Steve, did I get it right?

3.

When, Stephen, I dream about you,
you're up late talking, or directing a play,
or starring in one, or excoriating the bad
world from the Williamsburg
Bridge, or once you searched
for me in a basement where I was looking for sweets
Conrad exited to tell me I might
not understand war, trading, debt
and derivatives but I would touch them for the rest of my life
    here's some things I'd touch instead:

Seva's in a class, a musical group in northern
Russia or North America, in little towns
the teacher's cool, the students are mostly
Latino, Seva wants to fit in. Everyone learns
his name. He woke up excited to go to class next week,
            as if he relived an ESL youth in the Brooklyn 90s
            another time he found himself on stage
            he performed simple songs for villagers,
            shtetl people, and he performed the songs
            off cards, velvety red with yellow print on them
            cute, simple songs, played on guitar. He gets
            to the end but they want more, under
            a proscenium arch   or he was travelling back to
            Bensonhurst, where he grew up
            with troubled boys he played in bands with,
            who took him to strip clubs, who pulled minor heists
            his sister dressed him in baggy clothes, white pants,
            big coat   Selena was playing in the car,
            Amor Prohibido   he ran back into the house
            to get something, a kitten jumps on his shoulder
            and woke him up as a pillow   or he wore
            his Vivienne Westwood suit pants, but slathered
            in four patches of paint, dust, dirt and color
            on these precious, adored pants   spent an hour
            peeling it off and peeling it off
            looked in the mirror, saw four patches of color
            unchanged   he despaired
            but Seva, in fact, has great pants and they're fine
so the dream feeds itself on waste and love
and we meteors in each other's lives crash
the atmosphere and change everything
terrified it might not have happened, terrified,
too, to not be ready or enough
it's soundtracked by, if not Selena,
Sade, or Heavy D   what *are* we gonna do with it

Subject it to our discipline?
In Patrick's infrastructure dream
we've rented an abnormally large
house in the Pines.
Patrick's the first tenant there, but guests
swarm, cringey people and union
cranks with secret musical theatre
tendencies, crowding the piano,
taking up room in the beds. Patrick
keeps track of the tenants, then he has
nowhere to sleep. I dream of an extra
room in my apartment—a structure that
obsesses Patrick. He'll say, "You know
the dream you have where you discover
a new room in your house?" Well, do you?
He says it's a common vision. It relates
to epiphany. You habituate yourself to what
was already there, but you didn't know. It's a history
of the future: if what will be comes out of what is,
then what is to be done with what we have right now?
Subject it to our practice? In my dream the extra
room has an occupant, oh, it's Hannah Black.
Under the circumstances, her presence
is perfectly normal. Now it's my
turn to assign rooms in the Fire
Island house: one for me, one for Patrick, one
for a culture editor. There's a tender soul with a big
beard. He's upset he doesn't have the right
amount of cake, in a special cake he ordered
from the landlord, who's also selling us weed.
My cake's fine, I say—
to reassure him? He leaves and I find
a card that reads "Dusty Chain Police,"
I think it's his band?

In this one, I've got a superpower:
I can juice any moment for its maximum
pleasure. It's not chasing the dragon,
it's riding one like a flatchested, animated girl.
I'm travelling with Seva in disguise,
he's convinced we can't fuck on the rocks.
I'm naked and high on something,
irresponsible, symptomatic, also
cleaning houses in motion while we hike
great distances over the rocks
so he can finally fuck me in a resting place.
I don't recognize Seva, so I go on context
clues. Patito and Patrick are walking behind
me, I've forgotten long underwear, I can't
find Seva. We're walking over beautifully
cold ice so I can answer the door.
Am I too naked to make plans?
We're racing down trails to different rentals
in large rabbit burrows. We need to clean
up but we're so hungry, so horny and so
distracted we keep stopping to make
sandwiches or wrestle or—there's Seva—
kiss. Patrick asks me to look after someone
but I need to do it in the right order,
like keeping the right person entertained
with my stupid demeanor and remarkable abs

We're back in the Pines and engaged
in a long game of making two different
types of lists. At first we said we shouldn't
make them at all, but secretly we wanted to
so each individually made our private lists
and hid them from each other. One is
all words beginning with P. The other is forms
of painterly technique. We reconcile. We make
our lists out loud together, as if this

was this real release we had travelled for.
When we're back from the ice, the hike,
the rental, the rocks, PA, the Pines
we'll all find the words we left ourselves:
a perverts' future gift in the shape of lists and lists

Then I'm having sex with Seva and I come
so powerfully it's like a giallo film of
geysering liquid only it's actual semen
but I didn't remember the penis
or ability to ejaculate
I dream all the time about losing
my nails   it's sort of like castration
in the dream Seva's talking to me
in my sleep while he makes
arrangements with a woman, a businesswoman,
more professional than he is. I protest
how I don't want to use the new
system they devise, but then I worry
that my inability to tell him apart from
his business associate reflects my lack
of professional discernment
I'm trying to make it to Patito's house
there's a detour to an oogle apartment
I'm washing my hands in the sink, the water
is acetone and all my nails come off
I'd like to yell at the responsible
oogle but the residents are all arranging
a performance with the abandoned
pieces of a construction vehicle
now I'm having sex with Seva again,
my gym shorts are covered
in cum, I think it's his and when I wake up
I'm surprised to find I'm only
edging and all my nails are attached

Johnny's sex dreams are of the older brother he doesn't have
What about him feels like a brother?
He's familiar, Johnny says, He feels like my shadow
Proximate but distant, taller
and the sex feels like a two-player video game,
a symbiotic quality, almost like
Johnny's dreaming with another person
who's also dreaming him, so there's
two main characters re-dreaming each other
Johnny and his brother don't fuck, but they're naked
oh, wait, they fuck sometimes

now in my dream there's a swim
team of brothers, one of them's Keanu Reeves
I can't keep up with all the brothers swimming
they're in an underground mall
then I'm an accomplice to three murders
I don't feel so bad about it only I'm not helping
the murderer as much as I should
I guide him through suburban backyards up to
the disconnected segments of a ravine,
we're maybe in Toronto
he returns back to the original house
to complete the third murder, its victim a real himbo
I almost feel sorry for him though also I believe,
in the end, he played his part admirably

Or I dream of a noirish, zany plot in LA
I'm both set on carrying out
a plot and the subject of one   near-
misses and hijinks   targeted by a shady
ring of people, I miss their gunfire
by huddling with my "brother," my "brother"
is a pretend brother, actually he's a lover
willing to play a brother part only because
we're targeted so drastically
then I'm delirious on a highway
then I dream a lecture by Sianne Ngai on the zany
how it fits this case, instead of disappointing
aesthetic categories I'm fulfilling them, "flustered
exaggeration," Lucille Ball, I have to fact-check this dream

then Rainer dreams of their hands put to use
“in someone else’s sex dream”   Rainer, the dreamer
asked you what you wanted to do, you
explained that, since she was lucid dreaming,
it was “all in her hands”
I like this perversion of the lucid-dreaming fantasy
you pitched agency to a nameless someone else
I ride shotgun, my symptom drives me around
you asked my advice on dreaming in unison
in reply I only suggested the ecstasy of touch
in a minor place, the small of a back, the back
of a neck   if I author a futurist guidebook
of public symptoms, Rainer, you’ll be the first to know

Later, in a park, Rainer,
you swam with your "boyfriend."
You were teenagers. You combined
several exes into the composite boy.
He'd invited you to a relative's funeral,
an important step for your marriage,
with plenty assurances you could arrive
in your swimsuit. You and the boyfriend
arrive at the funeral as adults dressed
in swimwear, so you covered yourself
with one of Shiv's blankets. Your missing
cock was trapped in its folds.

In this dream, the cock will come and go
at will, like a regional accent brought out
by drink.

Then the collage boyfriend's
dad approached you at the funeral,
and it became clear in this part
of the dream that you were a known
alcoholic. "Would it have killed you,"
he asked, staring at the glans
on your rainbow-colored cock,
"to be sober for a day?"
Only the boyfriend's wearing
an expensive suit, the family's well-
off, and you and your cock have interluded
from the wrong class to hock cheese
to the funeral-wedding's lower-haute
bourgeoisie. Rainer, I read
your dream in the Mercer
St. Think Coffee, during my office
hours. At the time I worked 60-
hour weeks, and sometimes fell
asleep after class in the adjunct office,

under the table, so I didn't hold my office
hours there. Overheard: "It's a nice place,
a lot of people have second homes there,"
something about how hard to be
a staffer on the Hill, something about Cape
Cod. You have more right
to resentment, and it's so easy to resent
these people. Shiv saved
your relationship, see. He helped
you pick out new clothes, black
dresses and an oversized, heavy
black blouse covered in gold beads,
"like what an aged star might have
worn in the 80s." Who was old
in the 80s? Henry Fonda. Barbara
Stanwyck, who scams Henry
Fonda in *The Lady Eve*.
Would you make a good card
shark, Rainer, catching social
cues in your compact? But you
got distracted, forgot to return
to the pre-wedding funeral.
Instead you headed to the library,
tried to check out an oversized
scrapbook. The library clerks
rejected your ID and refused you the loan.
In fact, the guard broke the book
in two. You screamed he was "hurting
it." You got into a fistfight—to defend
the book? Thrown out of the library,
you returned to the funeral
of perfect suits, both you and Shiv now
in blankets and disheveled second-
hand beads. The boyfriend shot
you a dirty look—see, you could've
been his Barbara Stanwyck: forced a marriage,

snaked your way into property
by other means. Instead you realized
your toenails were too long, and removed
the toe by accident, then did the same
to the other side so they'd "match."
The cock is gone now. So are the toes.
So is the fort-da family

Jo, New York Jo, dreams of her high
school graduation. I'm there, but none of our New York
friends, not her parents or her family. She's back
in Ohio, in a water park. It's a real water
park. It looks nothing like itself.
One of the gays in her friend
group eyes a man in the bathroom,
some hot faggot pissing in the trough.
"Me being the girl that I am," she says,
"I try to play matchmaker," in the boys'
bathroom. You talked
up your friend to him, approaching him
mid-piss. But the cruised man
doesn't want the friend, he wants you.
He kisses you, he's still pissing—
to me that part's dizzy hot. Outside
the bathroom you make out with force,
slam each other into walls, knock into strangers,
leave for the woods to hook up. You pass by
a small lake with a fountain in it—Queen Elizabeth
is there, "in her yellow old lady
eleganza." There's a crowd—you pushed
through—you leave the ground,
like the vampires in the AMC
remake of *Interview with the Vampire*,
making out and floating in the air,
you're draped in the arms of her vampire
lover. Is that detail in the Tom
Cruise/Brad Pitt original, the vampire flight?
Jo can't remember, neither can I.
Her sandal drops into the water. "Fuck,
my shoe!"—the lover smirks and plunges the two
of them through 30 feet of air and below
the surface, where they can breathe and kiss,
and the crash, the cold, the shock of breathing
underwater wakes her up. I love, Jo, that I was present

at the start—a permissive figure? Cast somewhere
between madam and go-go for a dream
where a bi boy makes good on his promise
and, thank God, really lets you have it

Breaking down the dream, we arrive
at infrastructure: how it "sets agendas,
produces isolation, enables
cooperation" that some people
have and others need, including to be adored,
including to be schtupped
the word that Shiv prefers
or just to be regarded fuckably
Jo, you put the needle on it
KK said that Dannii Minogue did
everything Kylie did but "two years
later and in a porn way"   that's a lesson too

Sam, Patrick's Sam, dreams of Patrick
soon after they fall in love, "a whirlwind
time, but also solidifying": there's the eclipse,
there's New Orleans, there's New York.
He dreams of Patrick as his party self,
chatty and excited—riffing, probably,
unremembered riffs, with mutual friends. Sam's
helping somehow to organize the party, people
file in and fill up the space. He takes on others'
stress, solving "crises" that aren't crises,
as if the abundance of friends
and fun began, for him, to sour,
under a funk of responsibility. Then Patrick
pulled him aside to ask him serious
and necessary questions, about work
and planning for the future, splitting
finances, if that had been a problem in
past relationships—a mature
conversation at a party among new lovers,
which Sam dreamt Patrick initiated, and
then "waking up i found i had a huge
erection, and though it was very mundane
and even domestic, not sexual
at all, it was one of the hottest,
horniest dreams I can ever remember having"

I sympathize. I'm the one
who calls you perverts.
I'm the high bitch and I push
the button. You and you
and you have the excess
of desire. It's your surplus,
your turn to wear
the dunce cap, dunce
penis, your turn to swoon
for G-d the Father, my turn to trans
the kids. We're bouncing
a cock in common
space. I'm my daddy's
bony dream. Oh,
this is why I turned my back
on society. That's it. That is *it*

4.

I forget my child. She's 13 but I can't remember her name.
I'm at a sex party and there's a man here I want to fuck me
so I figure, like, she can take of herself.
My lover is older, lean and ropey. I feel some surprise
because he's both married to a friend and I thought
he was gay. The sex is pretty good till he starts
asking me about my kid—I realize she must be
pretty bored. Actually she wants to know about my
childhood growing up "on the peninsula" but I can't
remember that either

Now my family's in the mob but they won't
get organized   it's my turn to sign them
up for the amalgamated union that runs the Myrtle-
Wyckoff underground mall   when I'm talking
to my sister who's my sister and my brother who's
Uncle Fester I have to drop VHS tapes on their steps
on Xmas day in knee-high snow to avoid the attention
of the feds (the feds are children)
fuck, I have a kid in this one too
I introduce him to strangers at a party hoping
he'll say his name out loud and I won't
be humiliated by having to ask

Jeremy dreams he's in an auditorium
with a performer at the front of the room.
A child approaches, only the child isn't a person,
it's a wooden dummy, somehow betrayed in its
speech or movements or whatever. Jeremy
throws a knife at the dummy, which topples
over. Out of its remains flies, like a drop from
a boss in a dungeon, the correct translation
of Hegel's *Philosophy of Right*. Wow, we say, then
scold him: *Jeremy*! It wasn't a *real* child, he says,
somewhat defensively. Now everyone in the assembly
carries a copy of this translation made perfect
by murder which foils the plans of an evildoer
sitting in the front row. It could've been worse:
we could've sex-changed the—you already know.
It's a year of structured panic
It's 2009 and the world spirit got bangs

I'm talking cattily with Eva
all night about the dolls and non-
dolls   the latter small collections of shaggy
hair   there's a villainous creature
who needs fighting   a child is picked
as our collective champion   we have to
fill its backpack with water but won't it
leak out?   Then Hamishi dreams of drinking
adrenochrome   "what's that
drink they harvest from frightened children"
then Hamishi fell asleep and developed dream
pica, eating computers and vomiting
Lego in the mountains

I protect a 17-year-old
from Frank O'Hara, a murderer
he looks ghastly, sagging
from his freshly done deaths
O'Hara wears some kind of smock
his jowls drape nearly down to his cheek
his hairline recessed to his spine
the teen is frightened, we keep
having to shoo the prematurely
elderly poet out of the room where I'm
also asleep and Shiv's alarm is going off
in brightly colored chimes I'm not annoyed
or bored I'm taking the ferry back from Canada and Hell

Erinrose dreamt of a friend's
death she didn't witness. "I heard her voice
saying 'I think it's time'"; she watched a second
friend mow the lawn of a beautiful house.
Then the pace of the dream accelerates:
Erinrose stabs a different friend with a dull
knife, at her request. Still, the friend said,
it was difficult to die. Two huge black beetles
enter. There's a car accident, and now everyone's
dead except Erinrose and the beetles. She walks around
the wreckage, stepping in pools of blood.
Close by, a very young couple practice a ballroom dance.

Sam's in a horror-movie setting as a camp
counselor, Nazi teens swarm western Mass.
Sam runs away from the camp, down
long, sunny, palm tree boulevards in LA,
with Beyoncé, fresh from the Super Bowl
performance in New Orleans, 2013
the show and game and tourists crashed
the power grid that Entergy monopolized,
abandoned and left to disintegrate
So Sam dreamt of Beyoncé with the power
out   Nazis in the distance
Sam and Beyoncé run through "Scooby Doo doors"
cartoonish escapes freed from logic of space
except in "side scroller, almost Mario view"
catwalks, staircases in a warehouse
they exit out the back into a giant puddle
in pale blues, a small lake, almost Miami
colors   a dinghy awaits them in the parking lot
puddle lake   boat off into the sunset
like the non-dolls in *Some Like It Hot*?

Then I dreamt of a house that can fit
many people in a time of immense need
but it's badly scrutinized from the outside
and hard, very hard, even dangerous
to bring the people who need shelter inside
it's got a basement where I live with
a number of small and scrappy
characters, gruesome cisgender
puppets   plus an upstairs
of multi-level rooms covered in duvets
the upstairs can fit many people above
and below the duvets   it has a kitchen
that can feed everyone without limit
so: abundance inside, cops patrol the periphery?
it sits on a foundation of ice
it has a garden, inside the garden waits a troop
of watchful men, dressed like monks
they keep an eye on how people get inside
and how many, like local tax collectors
or the stooges of distant officials
or representatives on mission
in the heat of the Great Terror
still I'm intent on smuggling
people into the house: talking
animal friends, political
dissidents who take the form of other
animals like slightly obnoxious
versions of the Muppets
meanwhile an older woman lives
under the ice with a bloody mouth
the monk police warn me about
my smuggling, they're circling
the building, they'll be exact
in their punishment
I hide more and more people under
the duvets and inside the basement

I do this while the gardener monks'
backs are turned, I'm so successful
I could do it all the time
I'm so transparent I'm about to be caught
the old woman slips further under the ice
she's transmitting to us at a great
distance, she's hit her head
there's more blood everywhere but she seems
largely unbothered and I have the sense
these volumes will continue:
more blood, more monks, more smuggling
more people under the duvets, more food
in the kitchen's pots and more plotting
outside it   as if life were so linear
without opposition   as if forces
just develop under the ice
it's brick out there   I think I'll go scribble on a train car

5.

So I'm a pinched nerve
So I'm a stooge of experience
I'm sucking in air for a threshold feeling
like I dream I'm robbing a mail truck
as it passes through the mountains
Stephen's at Riis and his
shirt is off, he's doing pleasant things
with his face like raising his eyebrows
and smirking. Riis is Riis but it's also a wave pool
then I'm at a party where I'm not supposed to be
I'm sneaking in at 4 AM to torment
an incoming organizing committee
I'm taking dark strips of film and applying
it to my forearms as if it'll disclose its secrets
or leave an imprint like acid but as a tattoo
on the body, it goes like this:

Patito's in high school again, "an
indiscriminate school with very
distinct colored polos and khakis." Only
the students are all party friends
and Philly people, as if clubbing
was school and club kids the cliques,
shown to the camera on a ravey
cafeteria tour. But who are the teachers?
The dream takes a sitcom turn.
Patito's sitting in class with a sister,
"going brain rot for brain
rot," reading off memes and making
out with a boy from Pittsburgh
they haven't met IRL, only flirted
with. There's still the brain rot memes,
a homecoming game with the South
Philly afters crowd who sleep at odd
hours, if they sleep at all. Patito
tried to continue the dream—"I don't know
what I missed but I was Public Enemy #1
again" and there was a brick in their Telfar

Stiben dreams of a home for an extended family.
Maybe in the South. The dimly lit house
feels like a "placid version of *The Texas*
Chainsaw Massacre." Stiben's in a communal
kitchen. He's grabbing plates
and cups, intricate thick crystal with abstract
florals, he's clumsy at his task and
knocking things over. First another woman
checks up on him, then it's me—I tell him to shower,
Hurry up, I say, I have a surprise for you,
I start to rush him, I give it away:
Lady Gaga is coming, it's Lady Gagita
a blessed twink meeting Lady Gaga for his birthday
Stiben's not dressed yet, he's panicking,
he's grabbing clothes, he's
a rushed Little Monster, a Little
Monster missing a shoe. We gather
in the living room, we're singing
her songs, the real Lady Gaga's on her way
But we're asked instead to welcome please—
Sabrina Carpenter!
Stiben wakes up in mild gagged
disgust and he's late for a final

Zora dreams of an endless ki, in Tompkins.
Jo's there, Xya, Khaled,
Mateo, Ley, Sevyn,
Petey, Kai, Jesús, Nana,
Yesenia, Marwan, and I'm there too.
We're going to a reading at the Poetry
Project, and we're all in Telfar, the new
Telfar clothing, orange mesh
and cutout skirts. We're sitting
outside and talking
forever, say about douching.
Ley appears from the dark, she's
going to the reading,
and she's going to carry after. Where?
She's going to Basement. "We're all like:
fuck Basement, fuck Basement,
fuck Basement, fuck Basement,
drown Basement." Only Ley pauses,
hands on her hips, and says:
"I *am* Basement,"
which settles it.
Aretha Franklin's
playing in loop throughout the dream,
"with three Motown singers
in fierce bobs" bringing up the background
vocals. We must have gone to Basement—
in the final montage, Zora's exiting *a* basement.
She's hearing bars of Claustro
by Burial, the vocal sample that's like:
I've got my eye on you tonight
I've got my eye on you
and she says the dream was like a music
video, a music video of an endless ki
school without class
life worked through and labored
over enough it's smooth to the touch and nonchalant

"I've got my eye on you tonight."
Bobuq's travelling with a theatrical
troupe according to the stages of
the moon, to different landscapes,
and different states. Parents are present,
not Bobuq's parents, they're
white, but parents in the sense
that trips and friends amass a family structure.
The rain's been so torrential it's formed
a lake where Bobuq's swimming,
feeling alive and free and capable.
By morning the lake is dry,
but one of Bobuq's lovers
swims in it by accident and breaks
something. The two of them
pick up an Italian girl. The mother figure asks
Bobuq about their lover's dick, but before they
can really answer the mother shows
Bobuq a video of the Italian girl
jerking off their lover, and their
downstairs neighbor appears
shouting *Kamala for President*
and that's what they woke up to

I’m with Seva, Patito, Patrick,
only they haven’t met each other yet.
Patrick and I are trying to solve
the kind of impossible problem I call squaring
the circle, my idiom for a task that you can’t
either avoid or finish. We’re in the office
building where the afters is, but we can’t
find the office where our friends are gathered,
having more fun than us. Patrick
takes me aside to tell me something
important I can’t hear. When I try waking up
out of the dream he pulls me back into it

then I’m dancing with Shiv in a partial
room on broken yellow strands of either
glass that doesn’t hurt or stiff plant matter
if we dance in the right place with the right
energy and material it’ll create an interesting
effect like it has a name, a globe or glowing
ball, everyone’s trying to make one, ours
is especially pretty because it has no consequences
and to be sure we weren’t supposed to be dancing
in this half-sheltered bend made of driftwood anyways

and Rainer dreams that they wait with Shiv
at a bar in a mall to go to my wedding in New Jersey

Shiv has a recurring nightmare of a tsunami
he believes I'm conducting a tsunami
from the shore looking like Tom Cruise
in *Minority Report*, actually I fixed the dream problem
normally he grabs the person next to him, like his
grandmother, or Trisha Low

In a boathouse beside a lake,
on a lake in New Orleans,
Shiv and Elena are supposed to get married—
not here in NYC. I dream that this house
sails around like a swan in the water
on its own clump of earth. It's shaped
like a large, a very large, swan. Its wings
open at the back, the doors that Shiv and Elena
will process out of, from the courthouse, onto
the water, to us their adoring friends. The swan-
house is white and its wings are tipped in blue
trim. I'm doing reconnaissance on the swan
before the wedding—I watch it move in muddy
water. The back of it opens and rich people
emerge, not Shiv and Elena at all. We discover
it's owned by a bourgeois who won't sell.
We thought it was public, and it might've been
once, but he bought it. Elena thinks it's hilarious
and that it's not a problem, they'll get married
on the shores of the lake in view of the swan-house,
he'll sell eventually, floodwater will make him

In Eric's dream, Liza Minnelli's playing
Hillary Clinton on SNL
she does jazz hands and says *WAR Crimes*

like Joey dreams of Kylie
Minogue running for president,
we her fans were *terrified* she might win

in a different cataclysm Becca dreams she's
involved in an intense dom/sub
dynamic scene in the middle
of the combination French
Revolution and voyage of the Titanic
where Mel Brooks is introducing, presenting
and screening his latest feature
she's writing fan mail to Brooks
in reply receives a ripped package
of mass-market books and an empty
cigarette pack and now she's inclined to blame me

Then she travels to a city on the west coast
where I appear and invite her to meet my "mom"
in a large apartment. My mom is a script
reading of a previously undiscovered Brecht.
At the end of the play everyone pops
balloons and shaves their heads and I suppose
along the way the play, which is to say Brecht,
birthed me as well

Patrick dreams he's in Toronto
on a streetcar and looked behind him
to where Toronto Mardi Gras was happening
everyone dressed in "uh not right overly
produced looks"   and although it's a disaster
he gets off the streetcar to see it play out,
white tiktok people running upstairs
in a house to make a video
he's in some nonexistent west end neighborhood
going around a traffic circle like Spadina
but not quite that   he's fighting with his family
and his roommate's rearranged the furniture,
the cops are busting something   he kept
trying to take a video, "probably for Kay,"
to show how cringe and awful the Toronto
of it was but some of the
good parts from actual Caribana
kept entering the frame
in my dream he's on a blanket in my parents'
neighborhood in the Toronto east end
where I used to catch the streetcar
there's no traffic, he wishes things
were better and different from how they are
I'm standing on the corner and we're
watching teachers march, it feels frustrating
then we're going to a talk with a gay teacher
organizer and Bernie Sanders in a large
theater many flights down from
street level   Patrick's not with me anymore,
he's already in the theater with his organizer friends
I forgot to eat and need to do it out of sight,
that's why I'm lagging behind   I need a shower,
I need to find Seva   I'm so choked up I can't
speak   except to see and embrace Jo Barchi
to get there faster we throw our shoes down the stairs

Kevin's solving a crisis of party logistics
Seva had been curious either how to get
people into a building or prevent them from
leaving it, Kev put a party inside a party,
a kind of party inception, with rolling hills
and soft morning light and they're already
inside the space   it feels satisfying to crack
the code or solve the party mystery while another
promoter is catching the bill for the rent
in another Kev made a dub into jungle
mix whose purpose was love   I consulted
him on it as if there was something more, a secret
to be unlocked   in response to all my academic
questions he shrugged and repeated himself
I listen to the mix to solve two problems:
in one I'm working rapidly to disentangle fascistic
power over a small region of land, and while
our efforts are effective they're also exhausting
in the second I'm caught in a checkpoint in a different
place by the same rightwing forces that had controlled
the first   I guess they've come here after being
uprooted   I abandon the car with my friend, a doll
I don't recognize   we nearly walk into woods by night
off trail   she steers me onto a road that she knows

I want to organize a gallery show
in the middle of the final Unter. Chris is confused
at the idea and thinks it's one of my notions,
a New York indulgence or decadence. I think I'm
doing it because it would be iconic to write
about for the novel I'm writing, in the dream,
on raves and painting. Instead of writing fiction
about a painting at a rave, I intend to make it
actual, so I can describe it like a journalist, not
invent it like a painter. The painting I want is
composed with crushed black crystals. You can't
really see it in the fog. The artist tentatively
agrees but has qualms: how could he insure the work,
and won't high people crash into it in the dark? I promise
everyone it's worth the expense, I know what I'm
doing, I fool Seva about the secret installation and hand
out invitations to the party in the party on black
paper with the same crushed rock design as the painting itself

Emilio's exhibiting art in a fair. James
Fuentes, the man behind the gallery,
is a bubbly fabulous man. He's gay
in the dream, KT knows him. Emilio
hugs and kisses him and then he runs
away. He's exhibiting a plastic canoe
raft boat kayak, it's white on a white
pedestal. Raven-Symoné approaches
and recognizes him, wants a picture,
Emilio screams, KT photographs them both

then Joey dreams of Berghain, only
the interior was the lobby
of a Marriott (carpet, bed, lighting).
The dance floors for Berghain
and P-Bar were next to each other,
each 15 square feet—"*this* is what people
were hyping about?" he asks:
"Berghain-nova Civic Hotel."
A month later he dreams about it
again, only now instead of a hotel
the big room is a hockey rink,
the Habs are playing hockey.
The rest of Berghain looked
like a cave: rocks, grass, dirt, trees.
          I'm in the middle, explaining
House music to Kev, who didn't
ask for the lecture but doesn't run
away from it either   I'm doing it
"in German"   I'm at a party
where we're wrong to have fun

and Jo dreams we're throwing a Faggots Are Women
at Four Quarters, Pennsylvania
as if our church was fused to Honcho's
as if Brooklyn rolled in Appalachia
Jo's gay diva bio brother's there for the party
and the afters but he doesn't get it
thinks it's "pretentious and lame"
but Dominique Jackson commands
respect with her twin head prosthetic,
the Other Mother of the TS woods

Iris dreams of a week-long party
run by Ariel Zetina. We're about
to go to the Friday night Robyn-
remixes edition. I have an idea for a party
or a political action and an indestructible
but not camp news
commentator is going to interpret
it at a synthesizer, oh, it's Brian
Lehrer. He fucking tells us
what to do. I'm staying in a hotel
in LA. Grif Grif shows up
in Barbie clothes and a complicated
tank top, Cerine thinks it's a good one.
I'm at a party that's lifted
off the earth. We crashed it. It's on
a shuttle somewhere, hosted by a generous
brick of a man who doesn't seem
to mind we're not his guests. I dream
it's a party in the 90s. I regret the end
of the DDR but I can't say it. I'm
at a party in the "red dress," some straps
and flower appliqués. I see my thin
arm disappearing into a room. I come
get your honey out of a bag. I dream
it's Honcho. Patrick's there. It
has an upstairs and a downstairs stage, but we never
dance, just sit and kibbitz. Patrick's
pretty happy about it, talking gay
nonsense, we feel like teens. I dream
it's No Way Back. Zach explains
the party's splits and tendencies.
There are four main ones,
depending on which corner
of the room you start the party in,
and what sex you'll be at the end

6.

Flush with news Grace writes
to say "we were all leaving Isaac's"
to head to my house. Grace walked alone,
discovered the top of an apartment
building across from mine was on fire.
Grace tried to call to me to ask
if my neighborhood was burning down
as well but they were lying in the middle
of the street totally unable to move
except for holding the phone to their ear.
They don't remember a voice on the line
but whenever they tried to talk
about the fire all they could say was *consciousness*
is prisons too and woke up in that position

Patito's eighty-sixed from paradise.
Paradise is in the sky, but it's not death or
heaven. They carve out life on earth,
fight their way back to where they
belong, in this floating school or gay
utopia. The antagonist
is Charlene on a mic, stripping
Paradise citizenship and putting conditions
to its return. Paurro's there. At the climax,
a dance battle to regain Paradise, Charlene
dictating the rules. Patito gives a speech
before the battle about their ordeal,
wrongfully bootsed, unjustly chopped.
The room fills with people like a hallway
when the bell rings at the end
of class, an eager audience but no
conclusion, no guarantee, they wake up first

I dream of three union meetings I'm either
attending or making people attend
without me: one with IATSE, one
with SAG-AFTRA, one
with an electricians union I couldn't
remember the name of. Aaina
presides over one of the meetings. I head
to Fire Island instead. I take off my shoes

then Chris was given a job as a train
conductor on a line where all the conductors
are curators: Hannah's one, and Addison,
and Tracy. I'm supposed to be one too
but I don't submit the application on time.
The train is run by a university.
The team of curators, conductors and
communards is going to war with management.
We arrange for the destruction of a railway
bridge over a valley so the train will fall
and the university receive a fine. The bridge is
destroyed, the train falls, it's covered in white
paint—but the curators are blamed, not
the university, I think we're all gonna lose our jobs

A pervert's fellow traveler:
Patrick dreams of Sarah
Schulman chanting an original
number at him. The lyrics go:
I'm not a communist
but I am a pink prom-unist
he sings it with a fermata on the *I'm*
another time he's in a car driving
backwards from a black-bloc
squad of Philly queers   they try
to intercept his car but don't feel
terribly threatening   he wakes up
thinking how funny in the 2020s
the line from *Rent*   "to being an us, for once,
instead of a them"   then he's both renovated
and departed from an apartment with many
stories and high ceilings, I was moving
into it, apparently, quite soon

We're starring in each other's symptoms:
fondness, attachment, party
residue, cognition's hot
pink bag? Patrick says he's
excited about a place on Graham
past Flushing in a geographically
confusing East Williamsburg, he's never
seen it except on Craigslist. You have
to reach the apartment through the mirrored
back door of a liquor store to enter
at all and now he's worried
about the traffic   like his mom's
recurring dream where she signs a lease or buys
a house without knowing it's on a major
street. Patrick's new apartment is a punk
dormitory SRO for 20-year-olds who barely sleep.
Maybe it's the black-bloc teens who haunted him
in Philly. Maybe it's the last
generation at 538 Johnson. Patrick
tries to cancel the lease, but the 20-
nothings appear with a windup
doll of a stripper
dancing to an electric country
song in the style of Cotton Eye Joe

then Patrick and I are walking
in "Chicago." Police trail
a little behind us. We're
arrested after a slow-
motion chase. I didn't
wheatpaste this time, though
I'm grateful I emptied out my bag

Later I'm in a green marble
house. I'm showering behind
a green curtain. We achieved
our programs, a defund-to-
abolish trajectory. We applied
a new tax to stripmine resources
from the cops. I can't access the tax
cause the new organizing committee
doesn't have the right permissions
for the Google Drive. Patrick,
you stood on the far side of the curtain.
I felt self-conscious of my body, for once.
We trade verses of Celine
in French. I'm explaining surplus
state capacity to Aaina   I'm taking pictures
with Ben of two fabulous
creatures: a parrot in silver
feathers, yellow detail, a Morrissey-
like pouf. The parrot takes
a sweet dive in its pool. Its brother
creature is a Pokémon-sized bee
covered in a thick layer of yellow cakey
pollen dust. Ben says something like:
"He had a big day yesterday,
first he got castrated and then he killed
a bee"   I hear myself ask in my sleep:
which did he really do   did he get castrated
or did he kill the bee

Like pink proms and communism,
or NYC and wrong life:
a disjunction without answer
I'm only technically castrated, it made me
luxuriate   Patrick I'm dreaming about you again
I'm on a bridge or expressway, no cars,
people push forward   it's not a protest,
it's not bleak at all   it's triumphant
I'm trying to explain its significance
something to do with a tattoo
of a snake on my forearm and the pain of it
cleansed, celebrated by crowds in a distant,
solemn way on the expressway   I tell you
why I think it matters   you don't comment
or register a change   everyone's festive
and you're typing up the social forces
sometimes I'd like to see a smile break across
your political face   Michael makes you do it,
Lena   later I'm with you and some lesbians
we're accused of sexual degeneracy, the logical
next step is to do lines off the nearest available dog
it's a Wheaten named Max   you're mixing
everyone drinks and explaining how things at school
came to be the way they are   as if wrapping
the day's events in a copy of the Financial
Times, and the situation, you say, may
not be as bad as we fear

Then you were back in Germany.
You tried to take nice video stories
riding a train by the sea. Loud
teenagers share the train,
you're waiting for them to get
off so you can capture the announcements
about to celebrate your birthday. A travel
companion's kid runs ahead into traffic
on a tiny dirtbike—the kid lies in a walrus
costume in a parking spot next to busy
traffic. You're caught between taking the video
and rescuing the kid, afraid in both
cases that strangers would think the child
yours and that you bore responsibility
for its danger. In your danger, the child's
mom, your friend, was someone you
remembered from Die Linke in
Berlin, before the Sahra Wagenknecht
split. When you awoke you identified
her as actually Alice Weidel, the lesbian
former Goldman Sachs official and AfD
leader. In the dream the mom
was white and her kid was not and waking you
recalled that Weidel's wife is Indian and Swiss,
so I guess you reconstructed the logic
of a rightist swindle in your sleep for the Bens
Shapiro to wheedle about

I'm in the South with Patrick: we're organizing
something together, he tells me watch my
back for company muscle who'll try
to break the strike. I say yes but I'm walking
somewhere in a park in New Orleans. There's
a shock to my ribs, I collapse as if it's funny,
it's Patrick, he gently shocked me with a staticky
prod. Lovingly and with a smile he says that's
why I told you to watch out, look how easy that was.

We're on the road. I tell Patrick I'm spiritually
adrift. We're both going to the same city in the Southwest.
The geography's fucked, forgive me. Patrick
invites me to a Sacred Harp meeting, down a long
paved driveway and inside an old church. The pastor,
an older white guy, hands me
a sheet of music I can't read, and points me
to the part I'll sing. He must know I'm trans: the part
is for a low voice. I think it's a tactful
decision. I see Patrick on the pews, crying and staring
ahead, his face red and wet. A woman I don't
know is comforting him by holding him from behind.
He sees but doesn't acknowledge me. I worry that he
didn't invite me at all, that I misunderstood his need
for spiritual company as an open door. I'm worried
about the upset he experienced before I arrived, anxious
not to make it worse. Instead of engaging him I find a piano
so I can play the low-voice musical part the pastor gave
me and memorize the notes. The script's in bass clef,
I've forgotten how to read it. There are many small
pianos and none of them do what normal keyboards do.
I find a stranger, a young Black woman, one of Patrick's
friends, she reads bass clef and she's going to play my part
but the congregation's singing without me and I start to
work my way through the chords. Is it a song I already know?

Oh, you'll like this one: I dreamt
Ruthie and Craig repair violins
professionally, only they do it
as a front for the CP, in the 30s
Patrick I borrowed your symptom
then I witness a fascist in the Canadian
prairies but it's the 1920s. They offer
propaganda from the pages
of a magazine that otherwise
sells curtains. It's a May morning
narrated in voiceover from
Canada. It's the day before May
Day, it's technically April.
The narrator of the dream
asks viewers to witness dairy
farmers in Canada who drop
their surplus desire
overboard in a lake to drive
up prices artificially, it looks
like Cheez Whiz

Only I didn't invent that part at all.
Canadian dairy farmers
are dumping milk, I metabolized
the news   Patrick, you set me straight
about the milk   rigor for strategy,
power, the news, what's funny, what's cunt
what's discipline, what changes   it's one
of the shapes our love takes   our trust
fall onto language
      our learning play   our faggotted
love letter to people who might not
yet know each other but God are they going to

So here's my unpolitical travel dream:
I dream that the Degenerates—
Patrick, Liam, Stephen, Chris—
are driving somewhere
uphill, stopping when I ask for silly
reasons: I want us all to have matching
striped bathrobes, then I want
the bathrobes dry-cleaned. I'm writing
everyone letters in person
for a Xeroxed magazine on cardstock paper.
Later I dream the Degenerates are sitting
in the living room at the house
we call "the boys' place." Patrick's hammering
cushions onto benches. Liam
has his head in Patrick's lap as he works,
and Patrick's explaining that a revolution
in building benches by attaching
cushions to wood had led to a revolution
in the construction of chairs.
The chairs are covered in elaborate
crimson. Some of them mute green
and black like designer carpets.
So which was it really? he asks us
A revolution of chairs or a revolution of benches?

TRANNIES,
by Larry Kramer

1.

In 1978, Larry Kramer wrote the novel *Trannies.*

It's a realist depiction of the modern bourgeois transsexual,

all four or five hundred of them. Every

character is introduced by her profession

and college pedigree. Like: enter Bunny,

35, of glamazon proportions, with honors from Columbia,

an editorship at FSG, and a view of the East

River from her Kent Ave., Williamsburg, apartment. They are all un-
earthly shades

of beautiful, except the very wealthy and the (occasional) very poor.

They boast vanity in proportion to how beautiful

they are, and they all have time on their hands—

to scheme, schtup, fall in and out

of love, and mostly to party, which they do with the

religious devotion of wives wrapping their hair

for mass. Kramer lifts the trannies'

arms over their heads and wriggles them into beaded,

stoned or feathered garments. He works sweat onto their stately brows;
he watches them douche, epilate and fuck.
Mostly fuck: they're very proficient.
Their insides are ribbons of satin.
Their hands and mouths are trained for Olympic feats.
Some of them top, and those trannies are in high demand,
both among the chasers who flock like flightless
birds around them, and to other trannies of the satiny ribbon variety.
They have names like Fleur-de-lys,
Babe, Fanny, Velveteen or Absolut Puss.
Kramer despairs of their pursuits.
Most work in arts and culture, some in law
and some in medicine. A number of far-sighted
trannies work in the burgeoning field of computing. What
a nice decade they'll have. Some highly
successful DJs, experimental synth artists,
tenure-track or tenured academics, painters and critics
of painters and writers paid

for writing round out his figure. Some just roller-

skate into magazines; fame drops on them like a gag piano.

A couple are genuine celebrities, though the way

Kramer writes, every tranny earns her limelight.

They're extremely cunt and every Fleur or Poussé knows it.

For the purposes of this poem, Kramer isn't a tranny at all.

2.

In 2016 we used to say: I'm a faggot till I die!

As if someone had typeset it in small caps.

We meant it metaphorically, so now you have to

consider 5-6 trannies using a metaphor.

We said it in various weights

of mesh, and some of us said it making choices we later

thought of as youthful,

like highly pigmented glitter.

Actually for 3-5 months we all wore tattoo chokers, as a joke,

until it became possible to spot another

tranny at a party based on her tattoo choker, or your tattoo

choker, which also assured both of you that you were at the right

party. Then one of you nervously stripped

hers off, to be the less conspicuous

tranny at the party that was porous

enough to trannies to have at least two of you, but in mixed

enough company that you formed a narrow and missable
quotient, scooped together in a corner, or pointedly
avoiding eye contact, two high-octane personalities
holding court on opposite barstools to competing
and rapt clusters of a non-tranny entourage
though later, when you and the cluster had
departed, you'd say: oh, I totally
know who she is, we're mutuals but we've never
really met IRL, didn't she date that girl Juno, and someone
else says: which Juno? And a third adds: that girl goes
by Ghost now. Or maybe you were
at the other kind of party, whose vibrating
participants are almost entirely trannies of the five
to seven currently popular tranny configurations.
At that party you didn't wear the choker at all.
You might be more likely to end up in the corner
with the other girl, assessing each other or necking like teens
about to die in a B movie. You might have come with a boyfriend;

if your boyfriend is trans, he's probably outside peeking
at the nearby Grindr squares. If he's cis, then you,
who never pass up a chance to peacock,
are here to peacock: you want the trannies
at the tranny party to know that you landed a prize,
say a gauntly handsome punk boy with dirt
under his fingers, or a tradey snack with a chest
piece of splayed wings, who quietly worships you and fucks
like a machine, and even takes a slice of pride
in appearing in the role of a party sidekick
while your charisma builds to Earth Mother proportions.
In that case the girl glancing almost
involuntarily in your direction may be plotting
whether and how to make out with your cisgender
boy candy, to prove that she can, even to spirit
him into the bathroom at Mood Ring—this party
could be anywhere but it's probably at Mood Ring—testing his
particular devotion to you versus his general

attachment to form and genre, in this case of a waifish

girl in a slip sucking his cock in a bar

bathroom without a toilet seat. In the tranny terms

of engagement this checks out, as does holding

a grudge against that bitch forever, or waltzing

in to reassert control, and letting go of her infraction

with an almost tyrannical indulgence. If, on the other

hand, you came stag to either the tranny or the non-

tranny party, you probably checked out the available

goods like Madeline Kahn picking her stable in *History of the World, Part 1*, pitching herself higher and higher while the camera

rolls on its dolly down a line of plump Roman

asses, and in that case, too, you actively stunt

on the competition, either as the tranny who's had

the most tranny work done, in which case you're

wearing a garment flush enough to your front to leave

no question whether or not your tuck

is a permanent install, or as the tranny who has

the self-possession and/or bone structure not to care.

In this arms race nobody gets out

alive and nobody wants to, least of all

the trannies themselves.

But why did we say it?

For some of us, it applied as a straightforward

fact, if anyone can be described

as an actually existing faggot. We grasped it with a sense

of "finally succeeding in looking like others" (Hardwick,

who wasn't a tranny), and we felt that the empirical

faggots among us, trading Lou Sullivan

buttons and approaching leather like monks in their cells

might practice matins, earned their occasional smugness.

Others tripped into a pleasant abjection,

which they hadn't known to lay claim to before, and which

clung so tightly to their pastel lipsticks, makeup

staches and mullets fresh out of the box

that they found after a while they couldn't shake it loose.

Still others said it with a firm possessiveness
over willfully discarded flesh, living
or attempting to live the aspirations
of an eclipsed category like "crazy queens
who went too far." To us it sounded like something
out of Larry Kramer's *Faggots*, which holds in juicy contempt
the outsized characters, mostly Black, who won't
de-drag into boy names and faces, not even in the Meat Rack,
the navel of Kramer's personal faggot hell.
In Kramer's calculus, is it more faggotted to be *en*
femme until you get properly railed, or to clutch
after a sexless but infinitely more glamorous state like
going full-time? He dodges the question, and heads
back to his scolding chair.
Those of us who could be described as non-
empirical faggots, faggots not of this
world but the next, said what we said out of:
A) a desperate attachment to sin, which we believed in,

and which *faggot* with its air of willful depravity appeared
to offer better than the definitely more pornified *tranny*;
B) haughty self-preservation; or
C) sunburnt contempt for former lovers still
pumping blood at Golden Boys USA.
Oh, I made it sound like a gym.
We held in equal contempt the chasers who secretly
believed that wanting to fuck us made them
kind of gay, so you could say our former
lovers refused to see in us the phantasm
that our current lovers palpated, and in exemplary
tranny tradition, we spited them both, wrenching where
possible the cum out of their bones and sending up
our fervent prayers to see them buried up to their necks
in Hell's hot sand, like plaintive NPCs in a video game
level we could unlock, beat and leave behind
while they spawned, brunched, perished and spawned again.

3.

Faggots, by Larry Kramer, is a highly

religious and basically devout book.

I'm almost tempted to say Catholic, in its rapturous

attention to the body, the fetish it makes

of its many beautiful corpses, though *Faggots* is also largely

a satire of a gay Jewish man, edging on 40, in broad outline similar to

Kramer himself, I mean, he's got an Oscar.

Faggots has a worshipful attachment to the male sex,

so worshipful that in writing his carnival of bodies

worming, panting and pushing their way

into an Inferno dressed up as the Loft,

Kramer nearly, but not entirely, neglects

to add a couple girls, and the ones who crash-

land in his novel come in two flavors: Jewish,

wealthy, old, and tetchy; indigent, Black,

clever and recognizably trans. For

his part Kramer probably grouped the latter

in with faggot extremity, so it's likely, although

he wrote us into his ungenerous cosmos, that Larry

Kramer didn't know from trannies. His fools line the curb to get

into Hell, whither Kramer's Oscar-

winning self-insert dutifully tiptoes like a pilgrim

absent Virgil: horny, sober, sad, and ISO the epiphany

he eventually trawls out of a river of piss, all while his screaming

queens gleefully descend the rungs of an increasingly

scatological underworld. Kramer is a Dante

of other people's shit: part mapmaker of downward

mobility, part vice's rapt chronicler, coughing

up a pressed pill and taking revenge

on the fortunates who snubbed him

in youth, and in age would go on to landscape his Hudson

Valley home, by making them party upside

down in a toilet bowl. If it's a swirlie, why does

everyone think it's fun? Probably mass

social hysteria. Their names—"Boo
Boo Bronstein," "Randy Dildough," "Bilbo,"
"Dom Dom," "Dinky Adams"—really are
childish, as if skimmed from the age when toddlers
learn both language and bowel control,
and before they turn into trannies.
If you're a hygienist of the Pines,
everything's a cavity. If you're a latter-day Augustine,
Long Island looks like Carthage. That G'd-
out twink on the helipad might be God's plan, as might the
incomplete douche job you pulled last night, or
accidentally polishing your cousin's monster knob. Lot's
daughters passed up Sodom for something
more delicious. You get your rocks off and power up
today's harangue, and when, post-publication, the bitter
disco perverts stop inviting you to the nightlife you
love to hate, as indeed they stopped inviting Kramer,
you take comfort in feeling allegory

churn around you like a slightly less satisfying anal wall.

Reading *Faggots* is like riding a tour bus through a circuit

party where everybody's shitting in each

other's boots, except Kramer, who

piously goes in the bushes and comes out

the other side a changed man, without a Gabriel

or a horn to blow on, tapping at the gates of Heaven's

exurbs while, behind him, the despoiled souls on the tranny-

faggot continuum stroke their corrupted flesh

forever in Gomorrah and feel basically okay.

4.

You tried to write *fact* and instead you wrote *faggot*.

God made you do it, like He made

RuPaul tweet the trains flag, and atone for it

perpetually by indulging transsexuals draped

in blue and pink pastels like babies wrapped in cotton

candy. God set you up to fail,

and when you took a Xanax after

the underwear party in the Grove

and it bobbed in your throat

like a buoy, that, too, was God,

keeping you awake and making you look like an

ass in front of your slightly square boyfriend,

the trans one who, last time we saw him, was peeking

at the nearby Grindr squares and who,

when the swallowed Xanax melted and made you walk

like an uncoordinated puppet into bed,

remembered and cited this incident in his litany of
reasons to dump you, though technically—
anticipating that he had fallen out of love
with you in part but not entirely because of
your predictably chaotic use, in part but not entirely
because he believed that you
were laying down a mile of pipe—you got there first,
springing the jump on him when he got back from a car
trip to Montreal with his FTM bros and complaining
of his inattention, like a creature
who lives to be sensuous and adored,
under continuously stained cheeks.
We never see each other anymore,
you said, through heavy tears, and then
you made sure it was true.
The runny eyeliner is *not* God,
but the bellowing volume you reach
when you come gets pretty close.

So does the rip in your tights nestled

at the crotch, the one months later you got your rave

date to enlarge, to bite and tear at,

and eventually to fingerfuck you through

in an anonymous café on Nostrand Ave.,

near Sugar Hill, which first opened its

doors in 1979, when Kramer partied despite

himself, and which, while you and the

date throbbed on molly and you deep-

throated him on the dance floor, cushioned

your delicate knees. He's straight,

so under other circumstances you might

wonder what his damage is, when if ever he might

begin to suspect the degeneracy

of pleasure-seeking in the way you seek it,

and whether he'll resent himself for seeking it

with a distracted tranny, or rather recommit

to a profligate, non-natal thrill, and place it

on his mental list of tremendous

inventions like insulin, running water,

light rail, PrEP, Naloxone, the moon

landing, solar power, nylon rope and LSD.

Under other circumstances, you might wonder

if and when he clocked you, whether

it turned him on, what he believes that

says about him, whether he'll be weird

about it and whether when he tells

his friends he'll highlight or disguise

how he fucked a tranny right there where

God could see, and the dancefloor, and the DJ,

you might even have thought, oh, am I

still a faggot, theologically, and does it matter

if and when he thinks so, too,

but you aren't under other circumstances,

you're high,   and a sex change is not

a canticle. It's not a canto.

It's not Carthage or Balzac.

Actually, it might be a little Balzac.

It's not Delany but it's not not Delany.

It's not Andrew Holleran, it's a little Larry

Kramer. Do you think he ever thought about it?

I'm not saying Larry Kramer was a tranny.

Not even an edge case. I meant it

when I said: in this poem, "Trannies, by Larry Kramer,"

Kramer isn't a tranny at all.

But do you think he considered the idea?

If he did, maybe the thought passed through him

with a shudder, like you might imagine closing a

window on your hand, or maybe he felt a tug

in his groin, like a kid smoking his

first cigarette and thinking, wow.

ACKNOWLEDGMENTS

"Perverts," the poem, is an exercise in collective capacity. The poem collages my dreams with others'. Thanks to everyone who recorded their dreams for this book. An excerpt appeared previously in *Granta*. Thanks to the editors.

"TRANNIES, by Larry Kramer" was a joke before it was a poem. As a poem, it first appeared in print in *baest*; thanks to the editor, Noah Ross. Then it became a performance: at Sarah Schulman's First Mondays series at Performance Space, at UC Berkeley's Lunch Poems series, and at La MaMa ETC's Squirts 2024. Thanks to the staff and organizers.

Faggots Are Women is a party in Brooklyn.

Love and thanks to: Lena Pervez Afridi, Ryker Allen, Khaled Alsenan, Aaina Amin, Tyler Ashley, Yasmine Batniji, Jo Barchi, Joss Barton, Arewà Basit, Michael Belt, Chris Berntsen, Alexa Jo Berry, Sebastjan Brank, Anu Biswas, Hannah Black, Rocío Cauldron, Kyle Carrero Lopez, Chris Collado, Elena Comay del Junco, Maxe Crandall, Chris Cruse, Kyle Dacuyan, Máti Flores, Zach Fruit, Mike Funk, Breakfast Garbowski, Heather Glynis, Rainer Diana Hamilton, Nile Harris, Adelita Husni-Bey, Charlene Incarnate, Stephen Ira, Disha Karnad Jani, Kevin Jeffries, Capri Jones, Zora Jade Khiry, Kiwi, Eric Kostiuk Williams, Shiv Kotecha, Kriss Li, Sevyn Love, Lysis (Ley), Emilio Martínez Poppe, Patito Boots Martinez, Ben Miller, Ty Mitchell, Colin Murphy, Edwin Nasr, Liam O'Brien, Josh Pavan, Mythri Prasad-Aleyamma, Christian Prince, Liora O'Donnell Goldensher, Joey Regan, Macy Rodman, Tracy Rosenthal, Basyma Saad, Jasmine Sanders, Bobuq Sayed, Diamond Simpson, Amaryah Shaye, Eric Shethar, Río Sofia, Vince Tao, Virgil Taylor, Serena Tea, Rebecca Teich, Sam Tully, Stiben Vargas, Addison Vawters, Harron Walker, Maxi Wallenhorst, Xya, Iris Zhang.

Bottomless gratitude for everyone at Nightboat.

Marcus Berns, Cecilia Gentili, Z"L.

To Seva Granik, my whole heart.

Perverts, and "Perverts," are for Patrick DeDauw. I love being alive with you.

Kay Gabriel is a writer and organizer. She's the author of *Kissing Other People or the House of Fame* (2023) and *A Queen in Bucks County* (2022), both from Nightboat. She's the Editorial Director at the Poetry Project and lives in New York City.

NIGHTBOAT BOOKS

Nightboat Books, a nonprofit organization, seeks to develop audiences for writers whose work resists convention and transcends boundaries. We publish books rich with poignancy, intelligence, and risk. Please visit nightboat.org to learn about our titles and how you can support our future publications.

The following individuals have supported the publication of this book. We thank them for their generosity and commitment to the mission of Nightboat Books:

Kazim Ali • Anonymous (4) • Ava Aviva Avnisan • Jean C. Ballantyne • Will Blythe • V. Shannon Clyne • Theodore Cornwell • Ulla Dydo Charitable Fund • Gisela Gamper • Photios Giovanis • Amanda Greenberger • David Groff • Parag Rajendra Khandhar • Katy Lederer • Shari Leinwand • Elizabeth Madans • Ricardo Maldonado • Ethan Mitchell • Caren Motika • Elizabeth Motika • Asker Saeed • The Leslie Scalapino - O Books Fund • Amy Scholder • Thomas Shardlow • Benjamin Taylor • Jerrie Whitfield & Richard Motika • Clay Williams

This book is made possible, in part, by grants from the New York City Department of Cultural Affairs in partnership with the City Council and the New York State Council on the Arts Literature Program.